boundless
grace

LOIS CARTER

boundless
grace

Devotions from a Caregiver's Heart

TATE PUBLISHING *& Enterprises*

Published by Tate Publishing & Enterprises, LLC
127 E. Trade Center Terrace | Mustang, Oklahoma 73064 USA
1.888.361.9473 | www.tatepublishing.com

Tate Publishing is committed to excellence in the publishing industry. The company reflects the philosophy established by the founders, based on Psalm 68:11,
"The Lord gave the word and great was the company of those who published it."

Book design copyright © 2010 by Tate Publishing, LLC. All rights reserved.
Cover design by Kellie Southerland
Interior design by Scott Parrish

Published in the United States of America

ISBN: 978-1-61663-500-8
1. Religion, Christian Life, Devotional
2. Religion, Christian Life, Family
10.06.30

DEDICATION

To my dear mother, Freda Stiles, better known as GG—short for great-grandmother.

To *all* caregivers who labor from a loving heart, with or without monetary compensation.

To Dr. John T. O'Connor, a truly dedicated doctor who loves and respects the elderly.

ACKNOWLEDGMENTS

Special recognition and loads of love to the outstanding caregivers who graciously touched my life and GG's: Ruby, Rose, Pearl, Connie, and Clarissa.

PREFACE

If you are a caregiver of those who are physically or mentally unable to care for themselves, please be encouraged. God's grace is already on the way to help navigate the bumpy roads ahead. While you may be unable to stop what is presently in progress, you can meet it head-on with supernatural confidence because of the trustworthy words of Jesus, who said: "These things I have spoken to you, that in Me you may have peace. In the world you will have tribulation; but be of good cheer, I have overcome the world" (John 16:33).

Be of good cheer? Yes. In other words, "Cheer up!" God understands what you are going through—He knows how hard it is. Therefore, His presence and grace will go with you as you ride out the turbulent storms together until they subside.

He did it for me as my mother and I progressed through her difficult stages of dementia. I pray this month-long devotional will bless you with an enlarged view of God's amazing grace! It may be read in one sitting or broken down to correspond with each day of the month.

TIMES LIKE THESE

by Lois Carter

Times when friends can't comfort you
Times when human hands won't do
Times when good days seem so few
Times like these grace sees you through

Times when heartache presses down
Times when answers can't be found
Times you stand on shaky ground
Times like these God's grace abounds

Times when life seems so unfair
Times your load is hard to bear
Times you need someone to care
Times like these God's grace is there

Grace, oh, grace! God's amazing grace
Let it flow over you; fill each empty space
He will hold you in His own embrace
And kiss every tear on your face

Spirit of Grace

Looking unto Jesus, the author and finisher of our faith, who for the joy that was set before Him endured the cross, despising the shame, and has sat down at the right hand of the throne of God.

Hebrews 12:2

My ninety-year-old mother, whom we all call GG, lives with me and has advanced dementia. It is often assumed she has Alzheimer's disease because she can no longer think clearly, reason, or live independently. It's important, however, to understand the difference and recognize that dementia means a group of symptoms; it is not the name of a disease. It means an impairment of mental powers, *not crazy!* Alzheimer's disease is a form of irreversible dementia that progresses gradually from forgetfulness to total disability.

When GG's forgetfulness and strange behavior began to surface several years ago, it took a while before we all took our heads out of the sand, shook off the grit, and stepped out of our comfort zones. It changed our lives forever!

Who can we turn to but You, Lord, when we face such times as these? Just as GG looks to me for meeting her needs, I look to You for courage to face what I must face and to get through it by Your grace. As our Savior, You endured the grimmest of circumstances and won the victory so that we might learn how to give ourselves away in devoted love to others. Please give us strength to endure what lies ahead and assurance that joy still awaits us.

Truth and Grace

Be anxious for nothing, but in everything by prayer and supplication, with thanksgiving, let your requests be made known to God; and the peace of God which surpasses all understanding will guard your hearts and minds through Christ Jesus.

Philippians 4:6–7

Living with a person who is tormented by symptoms of dementia can be sad and disheartening. GG used to get so upset when she would misplace things and then imagine someone was stealing them. Since the two of us lived in the same house, I was probably the prime suspect of her stolen goods, though she never accused me. She was, however, sometimes suspicious of the grandchildren who visited often.

Of course, she always found her misplaced items in due time, but while they were missing, we were both a little anxious. I learned soon enough that it did no good to reason with her or to try to defend my loved ones. That only made matters worse. So I tried to stay calm, and I talked to the Lord a lot!

Only someone who's been there understands how it feels to be falsely accused, Lord. Lies led Jesus to the cross. Now people incorrectly blame You for all the catastrophes, disasters, and diseases coming upon the world, yet Your grace continues to abound toward us. I need to remember that GG wasn't playing mind games with me. She really, really believed what her brain told her, even when it fed her wrong information.

Courageous Grace

For God has not given us a spirit of fear, but of power and of love and of a sound mind.

2 Timothy 1:7

After living with GG's dementia for several years, I reached the point that I feared for her life. One of her greatest passions was working outdoors, raking leaves and broken tree limbs into a big pile and setting them on fire. Then she would work the fire for hours, pushing everything to the center, adding a little diesel now and then to keep the flames flying higher and higher! She was our precious pyromaniac.

Then one day, she got confused about the fuel and mistakenly put diesel in our riding lawnmower instead of gasoline. *What if she gets them mixed up again and throws gasoline on a bonfire instead of diesel one day? She could blow herself up!* I thought with horror. Thankfully, she told my son-in-law about the lawnmower before she used it, so he drained out the diesel and saved a huge drain on my bank account.

GG's strong convictions that she was always right confused me, Lord, creating doubt in my own good judgment. I didn't want to hurt her, so I usually acquiesced ... until I realized the dangers of denial. As I was of sounder mind than she was, it was up to me to lovingly speak truth to her and exert my power and will over hers at times. That was hard! But grace gave me the courage I needed.

More Grace

And why do you look at the speck in your brother's
eye, but do not consider the plank in your own eye?

Matthew 7:3

When GG started throwing temper tantrums and
bursting into tears for no apparent reason, I was
shocked! She was usually calm and collected—not
easily agitated. Extravagant with hugs and kisses
for her grandchildren, she expressed her love for
her adult children more often through acts of kind-
ness, not so much with words. She was reserved.

Over the years, however, she became less inhib-
ited and more comfortable in openly expressing her
emotions to us, just like an innocent child. When
she began reverting back to spoiled childlike pat-
terns though—wanting her way without regard
to others and saying whatever came to her mind
without restraint—even casual bystanders felt free

to supply us with quick solutions to our difficult situations. Thanks a lot.

Why was it easier to accept GG's bizarre behavior, Lord, than to receive the unsolicited opinions of outsiders judging our situation? Why did I try to defend my position on a rational level to those who had no clue what was going on? I was the one emotionally involved. They probably meant well, just as I do when I give my free advice to others. Please help me to grow up, put on a face of grace, and keep some of my thoughts to myself.

True Grace

Ask, and it will be given to you; seek, and you will
find; knock, and it will be opened to you.

Matthew 7:7

As specific areas of GG's brain began shutting
down over time, like glowing embers of a fire grow-
ing cold and grey, her agitation with herself and
others grew more intense. She became suspicious,
argumentative, defensive, and discontent with herself, with life, and with everyone in it. When she
didn't recognize her grandchildren anymore, she
thought we were all playing tricks on her.

After GG finally admitted things were not as
they should be in her mind, we immediately sought
medical attention. She was inspired after her
younger sister sought help for some of the same
symptoms: anxiety, depression, confusion, and forgetfulness. We soon received drugs to help reduce
her turmoil, with hopes of more miracle memory

meds for the future. She was given a short mental status examination of words and numbers that determined she did indeed have dementia. Time alone would tell if she had Alzheimer's.

Only Your grace could give GG a willingness to seek help for her problems, Lord. Thank You for opening that door of opportunity! The medications slowed things down for a while and gave us a few extra years of cognizant and quality time together.

Abounding Grace

When you pass through the waters, I will be with you; and through the rivers, they shall not overflow you. When you walk through the fire, you shall not be burned, nor shall the flame scorch you.

Isaiah 43:2

When GG started turning on faucets in the bathroom or kitchen then leaving the room without turning them off, I realized we could have a flood in the house one day. No big deal ... until working in the kitchen became a serious matter.

GG always loved to cook and bake for her loved ones and was very good at it. But the time came when I had to practically ban her from the kitchen for fear of her burning the house down. For breakfast, she usually warmed a sweet roll on a paper plate in the microwave, which seemed harmless enough. But the day she put a buttered bagel on a paper plate and tried to warm it in the oven toaster, I knew she wasn't safe in the kitchen anymore. The plate had turned brown and was ready to ignite by the time I smelled smoke and pulled it from the oven. I was tempted to scold her but knew she was clueless to the danger she had imposed.

When GG does foolish things, I try to be gentle with her, Lord. She has an excuse—her brain is shrinking. I have no alibi when I willfully wander away from You and create my own metaphorical fires and floods. Yet Your grace still abounds toward me!

Reigning Grace

Have I not commanded you? Be strong and of good courage; do not be afraid, nor be dismayed, for the Lord your God is with you wherever you go.

Joshua 1:9

GG and I lived together compatibly for many years before her dementia started setting in. We were both independent women who often did things together, but we each enjoyed our own private time and space as well. She was the most resourceful, self-sufficient, and self-sacrificing woman I had ever known. When she started tracking my every move, however, I began to feel confined.

When we were invited places and GG didn't feel like going, I was suddenly made to feel guilty for leaving her alone. Then I started getting edgy and resentful. It was so discouraging. We were at a crossroads. Her mind was playing tricks on her, and mine was messing with me because of my anger.

We were both terrified! Little did I know she was reaching out to me for a sense of security and stability while I was reaching out to God for the very same things.

Thank You for your commands and your promises, Lord. You remained right there in the middle of our messes, supplying both of us with grace, strength, and courage all along the way. Why was I so afraid? You always keep Your promises.

Visible Grace

But God has chosen the foolish things of the world to put to shame the things of the wise, and God has chosen the weak things of the world to put to shame the things which are mighty.

1 Corinthians 1:27

Living in the country with GG was often pleasant because we were both fascinated with the interesting creatures that roamed around our home. Our huge breakfast room bay window overlooks a garden of Eden with meadows of wild flowers, groves of pecan and oak trees, plus gorgeous green hills.

It wasn't unusual to see deer, wild turkey, armadillos, raccoons, and even wild hogs come up from the woods throughout the year. We kept binoculars handy for such sightings. But when GG started spotting people coming up from the woods in droves, it gave me a creepy feeling. I always looked through the binoculars to pacify her, but I could never say that I saw something that wasn't there. I knew her reality was her reality whether I believed it or not. And I couldn't change that.

Only Your grace could keep me from arguing with GG about her hallucinations, Lord. They were really sweet sometimes, such as when she would tell of the little girl who often visited her in her room at night. Who was I to say what she saw or didn't see? She loved her little silent visitor, so it wasn't up to me to steal her joy.

Under Grace

And He said to them, "Come aside by yourselves to a deserted place and rest awhile." For there were many coming and going, and they did not even have time to eat.

Mark 6:31

With GG's radical changes, family members became extremely concerned about the severe stress I was undergoing through my lone efforts to meet her needs. I had developed hives, a stiff neck, stomach pain, chest pains, sudden high blood pressure, mouth sores, insomnia, etc. So my family started pooling money and insisting that I hire someone to stay with GG so I could have some respite time.

I was truly overwhelmed by our circumstances but also clueless about organizations and individuals that served people in situations such as ours. Finding qualified caregivers was a difficult task. At the time, GG was still able to walk and converse a little. She was also fairly continent and not prone to night walking. She mainly needed someone to prepare her meals and monitor her meds. Though our needs were great, the answers were slow in coming.

The occasional respite helped me, Lord, but it didn't slow down the acceleration of GG's dementia. Still, I believed Your grace would carry us through, though I didn't know where we were headed or how we would get there. But You knew all the time.

DAY TEN

Assurance of Grace

Then Moses said to the Lord, "See, You say to
me, 'Bring up this people.' But You have not let
me know whom You will send with me. Yet You
have said, 'I know you by name, and you have also
found grace in My sight.'"

Exodus 33:12

Week by week, GG grew more possessive and
dependent on me for everything. I finally gave up
going out, except for necessities. Because she spent
most of her time in chaos and confusion, she lost
track of her days and nights and often got her med-
icines mixed up. It was a wonder she survived.

Coping with her challenges as sole caregiver
24/7 eventually wore me out. My body and nervous
system started shutting down. After several weeks
of sporadic sleep, I wondered if I would make it
through one more day. Sadly, I called her doctor to
discuss nursing facilities. He wasn't surprised. He

told me to take her to the emergency room at the local hospital for entrance and evaluation ... when I was ready. Simple suggestion, hardest decision of my life!

While Moses had thousands to oversee during the great exodus, Lord, I had only GG and myself to consider before changing her location. Yet, I needed the grace and assurance You gave him when you promised, "My presence will go with you, and I will give you rest." I had to believe it! Because You are faithful and true, I took Your word to heart and made the next life-sustaining move.

Sufficient Grace

And He said to me, "My grace is sufficient for you, for my strength is made perfect in weakness." Therefore most gladly I will rather boast in my infirmities, that the power of Christ may rest upon me.

2 Corinthians 12:9

You would think that after putting GG in the hospital for evaluation, I would get some sort of relief. Not so! She was so distraught over the change in her environment that I felt compelled to stay by her side. I was there day and night until a nurse made me go home, saying, "If you don't take care of yourself, you won't be able to help take care of her."

I finally went home, took a shower, and got some sleep. When I woke up the next day, I faced the enormous task of visiting nursing homes. Finding one that suited me and had space for GG was another story. What did I know about them anyway? Very little … except that our church visited one as a congregation once a month for worship services. I thought all the residents were sweet little old folks who did nothing but sit, smile, sleep, eat, sing, and mumble. Shame on me for my ignorance! I had a lot to learn.

I was no longer asking for a world on my terms, Lord. What I wanted and needed was to live peacefully in the world where You had placed me, despite difficulties. Would grace be enough to take care of GG's suffering and heal my heartache?

Faces of Grace

The Lord is near to those who have a broken heart, and saves such as have a contrite spirit.

Psalm 34:18

How could I have known GG would go over the edge while I was out searching for her a new home where she would be safe and sound? After all, she was in a hospital, not a dreaded nursing home! What could have happened? When I returned to her room that afternoon, I found her completely disrobed from the waist up, jabbering her head off. My heart fell flat on the floor! My prim and proper puritanical mother, suddenly a public exhibitionist! Oh! How would I ever get over such horror? If I ever needed God's amazing grace, I needed it then. How would I be able to live with myself?

In one short week, in that deep valley of darkness, God put His grace on every face we encountered. Each person we met was comforting and encouraging—from maintenance to administration and in-between—both at the hospital and the nursing homes I visited.

All my previous turmoil was nothing compared to the guilt I felt that day, Lord. It was as if death held me in a vise. I wanted to die! But I knew I had to shake it off and keep going. That's what GG would have done in my place. So I took courage, knowing You heal broken hearts. Your grace flowed freely in days to come.

Heartfelt Grace

Then Moses stretched out his hand over the sea; and the Lord caused the sea to go back by a strong east wind all that night, and made the sea into dry land, and the waters were divided. So the children of Israel went into the midst of the sea on dry ground.

Exodus 14:21–22

The first nursing facility I visited was the one closest to home (twenty miles away). It was nice and clean, with no obnoxious odors. Connie, the assistant administrator, was warm and compassionate—grace personified. But she had no openings. So I continued my search in the surrounding areas, to no avail. I felt as if I were treading water. Still, my family and friends continued praying for us and for a new home for GG.

A few days later, Connie paid us an unexpected visit at the hospital to say one of the private rooms would soon be available. My siblings and GG's grandchildren had already committed to supply additional funds to cover extraneous expenses each month above what Social Security paid. So the matter was settled. GG would move into her new home in a few short days. My heart overflowed with gratitude and joy!

Miracle of miracles, Lord! Just when I thought the world was crashing in on us, You opened the way for GG to get that private room in our favorite nursing facility. What an amazing stroke of grace! We walked on dry ground after that.

Grace for Grace

Then you will walk safely in your way, and your foot will not stumble.

Proverbs 3:23

Thus began a new season of life ... I visited GG at the home almost daily, for months on end. The majority of the staff were kind and conscientious, so she was well taken care of. They even catered to her by allowing her to sit in the TV room by the nurses' station late at night, long after others were tucked away in their beds. She wasn't fussing anymore. But she communicated less and less, so I had no way of knowing if she was okay with the situation or not.

My greatest concern was the staff's attitude toward the constantly sounding alarms—they seemed oblivious to those warning signals. When I walked in one day to the sound of GG's alarm beeping while she stood tottering (after falling and breaking a hip there months earlier), I panicked! They all apologized, but my only comfort came when I remembered what Jesus said about the sparrows.

The words of Jesus are always my comfort, Lord. He said a sparrow would not fall to the ground without Your taking notice. So I was touched by Your grace in bringing His words to my mind. I also knew I had to extend that same grace to those I was ready to pounce upon. Still, we all needed to keep a closer eye on GG.

DAY FIFTEEN

Guiding Grace

And immediately He called them, and they left
their father Zebedee in the boat with the hired
servants, and went after Him.

Mark 1:20

GG and I had fallen into a regular routine at the
nursing home. I visited almost daily, but came at
different times as I was told that helped keep the
staff on their toes. I tried to be there for at least
one meal a day to facilitate her eating, though aides
were there to help too. Sometimes GG could feed
herself; sometimes not. She was still continent but
had lost her ability to clearly communicate when
she needed to go. She could no longer stand alone.
I felt my daily presence expedited her hydration
and toileting by the aides.

Most of the employees were conscientious about
GG's welfare, but it was disconcerting to occasion-
ally find her sitting in the TV room with a little

puddle of you-know-what under her wheelchair. It happened more often than I would have wished. Still, I appreciated their care of GG and expressed my thanks by taking in home-baked goodies or finger foods about once a week for the staff.

Even though GG was in a safe place with nurses on hand, Lord, it was still hard to let go of her. Then grace led me to Mark 1:20 months later. There I finally found peace in leaving her with the hired employees at the home. Just like James and John, right?

Gift of Grace

For I know the thoughts that I think toward you,
says the Lord, thoughts of peace and not of evil,
to give you a future and a hope!

Jeremiah 29:11

Almost two years after GG went to the nursing home, I attended two funerals of elderly friends, back-to-back. Then I started thinking about a memorial service for her. I thought I was reconciled to the fact that she would spend her remaining years in one of the nicest nursing facilities in the area. When I realized I was unprepared to write her eulogy, I then faced the fact that I didn't want her to die in that place, as kind as the people were. Was there any way out?

After I prayed and searched Scripture for God's perspective, fresh insights began to unfold. It wasn't written in stone that GG had to stay where she was. My emotional and physical health had returned after a two-year respite; plus, her advanced dementia had moved her from anger and frustration to a place of docility and repose. Why couldn't we pick up and start over again at home?

Remember when I talked it over with You, Lord? You reassured my heart that it was okay to change direction in midstream, for grace would lead the way. You still had a plan for GG and me. What I needed to do was rest in Your ability to get the job done and follow Your instructions each step of the way.

DAY SEVENTEEN
Audible Grace

The end of a thing is better than its beginning; the
patient in spirit is better than the proud in spirit.

Ecclesiastes 7:8

The plan to bring GG home fleshed out more fully
in my mind as I prayed and searched the Scriptures. After I talked with a couple of nurses about
the feasibility of bringing her home, they informed
me of agencies that might help me. Then I spoke
to GG's doctor, who surprisingly didn't reject my
idea. I also consulted the local human resources
representative, who told me of programs that were
available to help meet our needs. We discussed her
Social Security benefits and other finances, which
revealed she was indeed eligible for those fantastic
programs. I had no idea they even existed.

After considering all the pros and cons and
finding peace with God over my decision, I set my
goals and informed my kids of my decision. They

were naturally concerned, but understood that *I had to do what I had to do*. If all went well, GG would be back home in the country in a little over a month.

Such serenity, Lord! I knew we weren't facing a bed of roses, but what joy it would be to see GG sleeping peacefully again in her own room. I faced the possibility of the negatives, but I focused on the positives. Besides, her doctor said if it didn't work out at home, she could always come back. Grace said, "Give it a try."

Great Grace

Now may our Lord Jesus Christ Himself, and our God and Father, who has loved us and given us everlasting consolation and good hope by grace, comfort your hearts and establish you in every good word and work.

2 Thessalonians 2:16–17

Everything fell into perfect place. I found professional caregivers who would watch GG on the side for a reasonable fee so I could attend church and other special events. I spoke with the dietician about pureeing GG's foods, with the meds nurse on how to crush her pills, and with the physical therapists on how to transfer her from the bed to the wheelchair and vice versa.

I made arrangements for a wheelchair and other hospital equipment to be delivered to our home. Everything was put in place with the agencies. It seemed that everywhere I turned I was getting a thumbs-up—everyone going the extra mile to assist us. Such a wonderful human experience!

No one in his right mind wants to give up independence to live in a nursing home, Lord. But when it happens, we all need Your comfort and consolation. If one is unexpectedly blessed to return home again, we need Your strength and guidance more than ever to help establish the work set before us. We need more than grace; we need great grace to follow through. Not easy, but definitely worth the effort!

Journey of Grace

> For the eyes of the Lord run to and fro through-
> out the whole earth, to show Himself strong on
> behalf of those whose heart is loyal to Him.
>
> 2 Chronicles 16:9a

There were a few doubtful onlookers when I brought GG home eighteen months ago; now everyone says they can tell we're doing well. We've settled into a way of life that suits us both, thanks to the generous help of others.

GG's stay at the nursing home was invaluable to us both. It gave me time to recover my health and learn more about her daily needs and demands. Plus, I met several professional caregivers there who give me occasional relief from my obligations. I gained a head full of knowledge about routine caregiving procedures and was able to observe the habits and idiosyncrasies of the other residents. Each one was totally unique and precious with both endearing and cantankerous ways. So it was always interesting. It was there I learned about GG's distinctive and peculiar changes of behavior in the evening called sundowners.

Thank You, Lord! GG and I both are at peace with where we are in our lives today. I draw on Your strength daily to meet her needs and take care of myself as well. You know how weak I am, but You show yourself strong in our behalf day by day. What a journey of grace!

Manifold Grace

A bruised reed He will not break, and smoking flax He will not quench, till He sends forth justice to victory.

Matthew 12:20

This morning as I sat at the breakfast table with GG, she in her wheelchair and I in my ordinary chair, my heart was touched by her feeble attempts to feed herself. Only yesterday I had to feed her every bite she ate. *Progress!* I thought to myself. I was so proud of her.

This ninety-year-old woman with advanced dementia has not given up on life. No, she didn't do it perfectly. Yes, it was a bit messy. But she did manage to hit the target—her mouth—several times. It thrilled me with delight. That gave me a picture of how the Lord, as my primary caregiver, may feel about my puny efforts to take care of myself. I see so much of myself in GG and realize how vulnerable I am. If the Lord weren't always there, guiding us by His grace, no telling where we would be today. I'm grateful He's not waiting for me to make mistakes. He's watching to rejoice in my successes.

My joy at Mother's baby steps of progress, Lord, reminds me of the pleasure You must take in my spiritual growth, despite the many times I miss the mark and make a mess of things in my life. It's all about Your love and grace. Thank You from the bottom of my heart for not holding my mistakes against me.

Touch of Grace

Then Jacob was left alone; and a Man wrestled
with him until the breaking of the day…But he
said, "I will not let You go unless You bless me!"

Genesis 32:24–26

As I transferred GG to her bed last night, her tre-
mendous strength in resisting my efforts was amazing. She can't stand on her own now, yet her resis-
tance is stronger than ever. It's as if she's fighting
against an invisible force.

I'm thankful God gives me the strength to
lift a body that weighs almost the same as mine.
Sometimes it can even get comical, such as when
she wraps her arms around me and both her legs
around my leg that I use to support her during the
transfer. If she refuses to relax her grip, sometimes
we both end up coiled together on her bed. I burst
into laughter as I picture it from heaven's perspective. Two grown women—wrestling each other—

one clinging and the other one trying to extricate herself. Sort of like Jacob wrestling with the angel to get the blessing, I guess. We are blessed indeed!

I'm so much like GG when You're trying to help me, Lord. While I cling desperately to old familiar ways because of fear, You're trying to get me to let go and relax. Sometimes the more You reach out to me, the more I war against You. Life is much richer when I yield to Your touch of grace and let the blessings flow!

Glimpses of Grace

Trust in the Lord with all your heart, and lean
not on your own understanding. In all your ways
acknowledge Him, and He shall direct your paths.

Proverbs 3:5–6

GG was mumbling to herself today as she sat at the
table. I actually understood what she said but had
no idea what she meant. She said, "I don't want to,
but I will if I have to." So typical of her when she
had more control over her thoughts and her life.
She was always willing to put herself out for someone else, whether she felt like it or not!

When I stopped to give her a hug later on, she
closed her eyes and leaned right into me, resting
her head on my breast. How precious! I wondered
what crossed her mind at that time. Since I couldn't
figure it out, I chose to simply enjoy the present
moment as it was: mother and daughter embracing
and resting in each other's presence. Perhaps she

was reliving days and years gone by when she was a young mother embracing her baby daughter. GG and I may have had a few flare-ups over the years, but grace always did "much more abound," turning things around for us.

What comfort to lean on You throughout the day, Lord! Your grace gives me little glimpses into GG's heart— the heart of an innocent child—residing in a worn-out, wrinkled earth suit. GG is still special and unique, though parts of her brain are now gone.

Energizing Grace

> But those who wait on the Lord shall renew their strength ... they shall run and not be weary, they shall walk and not faint.
>
> Isaiah 40:31

As I apply lotion to GG's aging body each day after her bath, I sometimes get fresh insights from God. Today I gently rubbed my hands over her gnarled and knotted hands; then I traced a trail of blue veins up her arm with my fingertips. My heart skipped a beat as I realized how thin her skin has become in recent years. But she's tough.

When I rubbed lotion across the scar on her hip, I had to smile. That scar is a reminder that even the best of doctors aren't soothsayers. While at the nursing home, GG managed to fall and break a hip. I was devastated when the good doctor, a reputable orthopedic surgeon, gave little hope for her full recovery after surgery or for an extended life. He said most people her age die of other complications within six months after surgery. Guess he didn't know our GG. That was over two years ago, and she's still beating the drum like the pink energizer bunny!

GG's veins are symbolic of how thin-skinned I was, Lord, when she started changing years ago. I sometimes felt battered and bruised by her thoughtless words. But Your grace flowed through others to comfort me and re-energize me when I needed it most.

Enduring Grace

Oh, taste and see that the Lord is good; blessed is
the man who trusts in Him!

Psalm 34:8

Meeting most of GG's basic needs is a labor of love
for me. Still, there are difficult moments, such as
when she is bathed and tucked in for the night.
Then before turning out her light, I discover we
must start the whole process over. My spirit sinks
momentarily; then I remember all she did for me:
from a bellowing babe to a tiny tot through my trying teens.

One difficult day, I offered GG a milkshake to
cheer her up and refresh her, as she always loved ice
cream. But she sputtered and spewed it out of her
mouth, spraying my hands and the table. What a
mess! I don't know why she rejected it, but I refused
to give up on her. I washed my hands, cleaned
everything up, and started over. When she finally

tasted how yummy it was, she wanted more. Then I got a taste of how good God is and the pleasure He takes in giving us good gifts.

You are so good, Lord! You keep on giving, whether we "get it" or not. Grace won't allow You to wash your hands of us, no matter how messy or wasteful we are with Your gifts. This cleaning-up business goes on and on, doesn't it? About the time I get it right in one area of my life, I mess up in another. Then You come to my rescue and clean me back up, from the inside out. Thank You!

Throne of Grace

Fear not, for I am with you; be not dismayed, for I am your God. I will strengthen you, yes, I will help you, I will uphold you with My righteous right hand.

Isaiah 41:10

As I guide GG's wheelchair, going back and forth through the house for her exercise, I hold her hand and walk beside her or in front of her to help navigate all the twists and turns safely. Somehow, this reminds me of the countless hours she walked the floor over the years—from one end of the house to another—bouncing fussy little great- grand-children in her arms, at all hours. Such strength! It must have been powered by love, for it worked magic—calming their fears and easing their pain. I don't know how she did it!

GG takes a bounce herself now and then when her wheelchair hits a bump where the tile and carpet connect. Startled, she quickly grabs my hand, then won't let go. She seems to find comfort in the touch of my hand with me beside her.

That's what Your hand means to me, Lord. Comfort! Comfort in knowing You walk beside us and guide us along the way each day. Just like GG with the babies, You know our needs and never tire of taking care of us. Thank You for the sacrificial love that flows down from Your throne of grace, through GG, and onto me and my grandchildren. We need not fear with You beside us, helping us and upholding us, as we navigate the bumpy roads of life!

DAY TWENTY-SIX
Protective Grace

"Do you not fear Me?" says the Lord. "Will you not tremble at My presence, Who have placed the sand as the bound of the sea, by a perpetual decree, that it cannot pass beyond it? And though its waves toss to and fro, yet they cannot prevail; though they roar, yet they cannot pass over it."

Jeremiah 5:22

With GG's condition, I have to be careful about what borders her pathway in the house. Like an octopus, she's forever reaching out and grabbing things that appear to be far out of her grasp. It could be dangerous, and I don't want her life complicated by more pain or injuries.

Bedrails also help serve as a boundary for her protection. She doesn't try to crawl out of bed now that she's back home, but she does roll from side to side and swing her legs over the rails. Great exercise! That's GG doing the rock and roll. When she's ready to get out of bed, she shakes the bedrail fiercely. Her shake, rattle, and roll gets my attention, and her gentle roar usually gets her out of bed on demand.

Boundaries! Where would we be without them, Lord? And where would we be without grace? We'd be lost without both. Personal boundaries help prevent broken hearts, broken homes, broken relationships, damaged emotions, and deep, deep scars. Grace allows a leash long enough to continually develop our spiritual muscles but short enough to hold us close to Your heart and under Your watchful care. Grace truly saves and keeps us.

Exceeding Grace

Come unto Me, all you who labor and are heavy
laden, and I will give you rest...you will find rest
for your souls. For My yoke is easy and My burden
is light.

Matthew 11:28–30

As I carefully lift GG from her bed, I'm often
reminded of how gentle the Lord is with us. He
daily bears the emotional weights we carry and lifts
us up from beds of anguish and pools of self-pity. If
it's a case of "I made my own bed; now I have to lie
in it" or if I'm down and out because someone else
did me wrong, Jesus is always there to lift me up
when I reach out to Him. His invitation is always
to "come and rest."

Unlike most elderly folks with soft and pow-
dery bones, GG has good bone density for her age
because of all the time she spent working outdoors
and taking in the vitamins from the sunshine. Still,

when she resists my efforts to lift her, I must wait until she yields to my touch. If I force my will on hers while she is resisting, it could hurt her and me. I can tell when she is relaxed and ready to let me help her.

It's the same with Your grace, Lord. You know when we're receptive or resistant. Is it because Your grace is so prevalent and free that we esteem it so lightly at times? Is it too good to be true? You say, "Come," with no other qualifications, so I come to You and rest in Your ability to do what I can't do myself.

DAY TWENTY-EIGHT
Omniscient Grace

O Lord, You have searched me and known me.
You know my sitting down and my rising up; You
understand my thought afar off. You comprehend
my path and my lying down, and are acquainted
with all my ways.

Psalm 139:1–3

Watching GG day after day has acquainted me
with the full gamut of her behaviors, including her
sundowners. That's when she gets more agitated in
the afternoons, making strange sounds and mov-
ing her hands in ritualistic motions—very common
among those with dementia. To help combat her
frustrations, I learned to keep soft toys and cloth
books in front of her to keep her hands occupied.
Sometimes I put washcloths in a small plastic basket for her to fold.

I also put photos of her loved ones in sealed
plastic baggies for her to see and handle without

tearing them up. I write their names and relation-ships with magic markers on the baggies; then throughout the day, I remind GG of their names, along with some memory I hold that perhaps is stored away in her long-term memory.

How great is Your omniscience, Lord! You keep track of our names and faces and all of our goings-on, yet You don't keep track of our mistakes. That's what I call grace! And You even like to be reminded of our love relationship with You. Joy! Joy!

Abundant Grace

Honor your father and your mother…If a man says to his father or his mother, "Whatever profit you might have received from me is…a gift to God," then you no longer let him do anything for his father or his mother, making the word of God of no effect through your tradition.

Mark 7:10–13

What are adult children to do with aging parents who can no longer live alone? Many are unable to care for parents at home because of geographic separations, limited financial resources, or restricted health issues. Those who work outside the home have fewer options. Sad to say, some sons and daughters are so emotionally scarred by parents that they are alienated from one another. Therefore, we must not judge others harshly when we haven't walked in their shoes and know nothing of their parent/child relationships.

Few of us would wish to impose on our adult children in years to come...or live in a nursing home. So what are we to do when we face that dilemma? If seeds of selfless love and compassion are planted within our children, such as GG planted, surely we can trust them to do right by us to the best of their ability, whatever their choices may be.

This roller coaster ride with GG has been scary at times, Lord, but I wouldn't have missed it for anything! It's taught me more about Your grace than all my other life experiences put together.

Amazing Grace

Being confident of this very thing, that He who has begun a good work in you will complete it until the day of Jesus Christ.

Philippians 1:6

My experiences with GG, from the onset of her dementia through her two years at the nursing home, followed a fairly predictable path of progression. Her loss of memory and independence over time ultimately led to my turning her over to the care of strangers (though reluctantly). We did what we had to do at the time. No matter where one is with his or her parents on the timeline I've shared, my prayer is that he or she will find hope and encouragement from my thoughts and prayers. May the daily scriptures bring God closer to each heart and situation.

Not everyone gets a second chance to do things over, as GG and I did. While our choice worked well for us, it wouldn't work for everyone. As I yielded to God's guidance, He poured out His grace on us and stacked the dominoes with perfect precision. Everything fell into place. I have no regrets!

When You planted the seed in my mind to bring GG back home, Lord, You confirmed it by Your word. Then all I had to do was let You work out the details. What an orchestration of events! What amazing grace! You started it, and You're not finished with us yet.

Rhythmic Grace

I will both lie down in peace, and sleep; for You alone, O Lord, make me dwell in safety.

Psalm 4:8

At the close of each day, I lay GG down to get a good night's rest. Once she starts relaxing and breathing rhythmically, I find my own place to relax and tune in to the heartbeat of God. What joy to see her let go of her tension in exchange for peace and serenity! When she lived at the nursing home those two years, she never got enough sleep because of its busy schedule, so she was often irritated and frustrated. Now she is at peace here at home, sleeping in her own bed, eating at her own table, looking out her own window at the beautiful hills and meadows. All her needs are met.

What a perfect picture of the twenty-third Psalm! "The Lord is our shepherd; we shall not want. He makes us to lie down in green pastures ... He restores our souls. He leads us in the paths of righteousness for His name's sake. Yea, though we walk through the valley of the shadow of death, we will fear no evil; for you are with us … Surely goodness and mercy shall follow us all the days of our lives and we will dwell in the house of the Lord forever."

*What a **fresh** old psalm, Lord! The good Shepherd continues to bring us abundant life and will until the day You call us home. Thank You for Your glorious grace. My cup runs over!*

TEN COMMANDMENTS FOR CAREGIVERS

I. You shall honor your father and your mother.

II. You shall monitor their medications.

III. You shall handle their fragile bod-
ies as gently as possible.

IV. You shall take nothing they say personally.

V. You shall not argue with them, scold them,
or correct them publically or privately.

VI. You shall encourage them to tell you their names
every day, lest they lose their own identity.

VII. You shall share family news and current events
with them even if they seem to not understand.

VIII. You shall not toss out all their old treasures
just because they look like junk to you.

IX. You shall see that they have a living will
and a do-not-resuscitate (DNR) form stat-
ing their wishes (signed and witnessed).

X. You shall hold power of attorney for
them or see that someone trusted
holds power of attorney for them.

Lois Carter

A FEW GOLDEN RULES
FOR CAREGIVERS

Thou shalt love them while you have them.

Thou shalt shower thyself with grace.

When discouraged, thou shalt remember it is the disease acting and speaking, not the person!

A DOZEN HANDY HINTS
FOR CAREGIVERS

1. Always have an extra key to your parents' or loved ones' homes.

2. If they talk about going home to their childhood place, put them in the car (if possible) and go for a ride.

3. When old items need to be replaced (such as recliners, shoes, or clothing), make changes as they sleep.

4. When purging the clutter from their rooms or home, do it while they sleep. Or ask permission if they are awake.

5. If they automatically say no to your offer of food or beverage, assume they really mean yes; then go forward.

6. Crush their medications (when allowed) and mix with tapioca pudding for easier swallowing. The bubbles in the tapioca help mask the tiny chunks of medicine.

7. Practice the art of touch therapy. Give lots of hugs, pats, and squeezes. They probably won't want to let go.

8. Honor the person you knew them once to be—in clothing selections (style and color), in food choices, and in their preferences for music and TV (or in their orientation toward silence and solitude).

9. Put pictures of their loved ones in plastic baggies, seal; then write their names and relationships with permanent markers.

10. Keep a basket of soft toys and cloth books within their reach to keep their busy hands occupied.

11. When overwhelmed by circumstances, call a compassionate friend who will allow you to vent. Talk therapy brings healing.

12. Above all, pray!

AFTERWORD

As you meet the physical and emotional needs of your loved ones, perhaps you would also like to be an instrument in meeting their spiritual needs. If they are willing and able, would you be willing to assure them of a personal relationship with God through Jesus Christ? It's as easy as ABC. Simply have them repeat after you:

Father God, Creator of heaven and earth,

I *admit* I am a sinner in need of a Savior (Romans 3:23).

I *believe* You sent Your Son to die for my sins so I could have eternal life (John 3:16) and share a loving relationship with You (John 17:3). Therefore, I ask You to forgive me of my sins as I invite Jesus Christ into my heart and life (Revelation 3:20).

I *confess* that I am now a new creation in Him (2 Corinthians 5:17), and I thank You that from this point on, we are bound together for eternity.

In Jesus's name I pray. Amen.

With much appreciation and lots of love, hugs, and kisses to Meghan Duis, GG's great-granddaughter, for capturing the essence of her great-aunt Lois and GG's relationship in the photo she took of them in 2009. We gratefully acknowledge her permission to use the picture on the cover of *Boundless Grace.*